Ins:
SUCC
LEADERSHIP

MW00812045

Helpful advice for those who are leaders
and for those who long to become leaders

Rick Renner

TEACH ALL NATIONS

A book company anointed to take God's Word to you
and to the nations of the world.

A division of *RICK RENNER MINISTRIES*
P. O. Box 702040 Tulsa, OK 74170-2040
Phone: 877-281-8644 Fax: 888-281-4686
E-mail: renner@renner.org

Insights on Successful Leadership:
Helpful Advice for Leaders
And for Those Who Long To Become Leaders
ISBN 0-9725454-3-3
Copyright © 2004 by Rick Renner
P. O. Box 702040
Tulsa, OK 74170-2040

Editorial Consultant: Cynthia D. Hansen

Printed in the United States of America.

Be diligent in these matters;
give yourself wholly to them,
so that everyone may see your progress.

1 Timothy 4:15
(NIV)

SUCCESSFUL LEADERSHIP

*For the eyes
of the Lord run to
and fro through-
out the whole
earth, to shew
himself strong in
the behalf of
them whose heart
is perfect toward
him....*

2 Chronicles 16:9
(KJV)

A s you search high and low for someone to help you do big things for
God and take steps that will shake the
foundations of hell, remember this: *It's
not a job for the weak-willed and opinion-
driven person.*

The above quotation is adapted from Rick Renner's book
Who Is Ready for a Spiritual Promotion?

4

SUCCESSFUL LEADERSHIP

I f people see you actually do what you said you would do — something stupendous that bears great fruit — the next time you announce you are going to do something outrageous and wild, they will believe you!

Let your light so shine before men, that they may see your good works and glorify your Father which is in heaven.

Matthew 5:16 (KJV)

The above quotation is adapted from Rick Renner's book
The Point of No Return: Tackling Your Next New Assignment With Courage and Common Sense.

SUCCESSFUL LEADERSHIP

If a leader has a life to back up his message, people will respect his words. But if he tries to tell others to do what they know he isn't doing in his own life, he negates both his message and his authority. The most important pulpit a leader possesses is the testimony of his own personal life.

The above quotation is adapted from Rick Renner's book
Who Is Ready for a Spiritual Promotion?

SUCCESSFUL LEADERSHIP

W hen I'm looking for someone to fill a leadership vacancy, I look to those who have made themselves meaningful, pivotal, and crucial — key to their various divisions. Why should I look to other pastures for leadership if I have such a leader right here in front of me?

And let these also first be proved....

1 Timothy 3:10 (KJV)

The above quotation is adapted from Rick Renner's book
Who Is Ready for a Spiritual Promotion?

For we must all appear before the judgment seat of Christ; that every one may receive the things done in his body, according to that he hath done, whether it be good or bad.

2 Corinthians 5:10 (KJV)

Unfortunately, believers are sometimes the most gifted lazy people in the world. Their eternal destiny is Heaven, but in this world there is no vast difference between them and the unbelievers. At the point of death, one will go to Heaven and the other to hell. But in life, they both did the same thing — *nothing*.

The above quotation is adapted from Rick Renner's book
If You Were God, Would You Choose You?

L eadership is *not* convenient.

...Whosoever will come after me, let him deny himself, and take up his cross, and follow me.

Mark 8:34 (KJV)

The above quotation is adapted from Rick Renner's book
Who Is Ready for a Spiritual Promotion?

He also that is slothful in his work is brother to him that is a great waster.

Proverbs 18:9 (KJV)

I f you bring a lazy, non-performing person into your team, it will prove to be one of the most frustrating experiences you'll ever have.

The above quotation is adapted from Rick Renner's book *Who Is Ready for a Spiritual Promotion?*

SUCCESSFUL LEADERSHIP

Y ou may be like one of the disciples — not naturally gifted or educated, but called and therefore filled with God's ability to tackle the impossible and to change the world.

But ye shall receive power, after that the Holy Ghost is come upon you....

Acts 1:8 (KJV)

The above quotation is adapted from Rick Renner's book *The Point of No Return: Tackling Your Next New Assignment With Courage and Common Sense.*

SUCCESSFUL LEADERSHIP

*Brethren,
I count not
myself to have
apprehended:
but this one
thing I do,
forgetting those
things which
are behind....*

*Philippians 3:13
(KJV)*

D on't make the mistake of holding on to what God has released.

The above quotation is adapted from Rick Renner's book
If You Were God, Would You Choose You?

SUCCESSFUL LEADERSHIP

B ad times eventually pass, and dark clouds never last. Eventually the sun always comes out, and the birds start singing again. Wouldn't it be a pity if you gave up and sacrificed everything you've worked so hard to gain just because of a few dark clouds?

Regardless of whether times are good or bad, that is your post, your place of responsibility; so dig in, take a firm stand, and resolve that you are going to be faithful!

2 Timothy 4:2 (REV)

The above quotation is adapted from Rick Renner's book *Sparkling Gems From the Greek*.

A great door and effectual is opened unto me, and there are many adversaries.

1 Corinthians 16:9 (KJV)

J ealousy and coveteousness in others often manifests when God opens a door of opportunity. Those with impure motives have a way of showing up wherever people are being blessed, so don't be surprised if it happens to you. Be careful not to let these types of individuals steal the victory you've worked so hard to achieve.

The above quotation is adapted from Rick Renner's book *Sparkling Gems From the Greek*.

SUCCESSFUL LEADERSHIP

C hange is always threatening to people, and new leadership represents change. So if you are a new leader, don't be surprised if people at first seem slow to respond to your new ideas.

And the servant of the Lord must not strive; but be gentle unto all men, apt to teach, patient.

2 Timothy 2:24 (KJV)

The above quotation is adapted from Rick Renner's book
The Point of No Return: Tackling Your Next New Assignment With Courage and Common Sense.

*Let your
roots grow down
deep into him
and draw your
nourishment
from him....*

*Colossians 2:7
(TLB)*

I f your roots are securely fixed in Jesus Christ, you will outlast every season, every foul climate, and every storm. When the storm clouds pass, you will enter the finest fruit-producing season of your life, your ministry, your family, or your business.

The above quotation is adapted from Rick Renner's book *Sparkling Gems From the Greek.*

SUCCESSFUL LEADERSHIP

N ew leaders, whether new presidents or new employers, are always compared to their predecessors. It is the nature of human beings to watch, compare, talk, test, and try new leadership. This is one reason why following in the steps of a strong leader can be a challenging and often frustrating experience.

There shall not any man be able to stand before thee all the days of thy life... I will be with thee: I will not fail thee, nor forsake thee.

Joshua 1:5 (KJV)

The above quotation is adapted from Rick Renner's book *The Point of No Return: Tackling Your Next New Assignment With Courage and Common Sense*.

*The tongue
of the wise
makes knowledge
acceptable....*

*Proverbs 15:2
(NAS)*

L eadership is *communication*. That
may sound too simple to be true, but
it's a fact that good leaders and bad leaders
are distinguished by how they communicate. Analyze the type of problems that
commonly arise, and you'll discover that
most of these problems find their roots
in *poor communication*.

The above quotation is adapted from Rick Renner's book
Who Is Ready for a Spiritual Promotion?

H ard work is required to achieve success.

He who works his land will have abundant food, but the one who chases fantasies will have his fill of poverty.

Proverbs 28:19 (NIV)

The above quotation is adapted from Rick Renner's book *Sparkling Gems From the Greek*.

Don't get in a hurry when it comes to laying your hands on people and giving them your seal of approval....

1 Timothy 5:22 (REV)

Promoting anyone too quickly is not wise. So to begin with, just give a prospective leader a little responsibility; then observe what he does with it. Years of experience have taught me that when you promote someone too high and too fast, everyone gets hurt in the end.

The above quotation is adapted from Rick Renner's book
Who Is Ready for a Spiritual Promotion?

Y ou can't experience what God wants to do *today* while you're still clinging to the past.

Remember ye not the former things, neither consider the things of old.

Isaiah 43:18 (KJV)

The above quotation is adapted from Rick Renner's book
If You Were God, Would You Choose You?

SUCCESSFUL LEADERSHIP

*Like a father
pitieth his children,
so the Lord pitieth
them that fear him.
For he knoweth
our frame; he
remembereth that
we are dust.*

*Psalm 103:13,14
(KJV)*

A big test for you will be to see how you respond to a leader's humanity. If you judge him for being imperfect, then you are not mature enough to move into leadership yourself.

The above quotation is adapted from Rick Renner's book
*The Point of No Return: Tackling Your Next New Assignment
With Courage and Common Sense.*

SUCCESSFUL LEADERSHIP

E veryone feels afraid to step out and do something new, so a leader must be able to impart enough confidence to people to cause them to take that next bold step of faith.

Be strong (confident) and of good courage, for you shall cause this people to inherit the land....

Joshua 1:6 (AMP)

The above quotation is adapted from Rick Renner's book *Who Is Ready for a Spiritual Promotion?*

SUCCESSFUL LEADERSHIP

Wherefore, my beloved brethren, let every man be swift to hear....

James 1:19 (KJV)

I've learned that I must discipline myself to *listen* to what people are saying to me. Otherwise, they'll think I'm listening when, in reality, I'm about a million miles away in my thoughts. If I'm going to hear what they are saying, I have to push everything else out of my mind and deliberately *focus* on what they're saying.

The above quotation is adapted from Rick Renner's book *Sparkling Gems From the Greek.*

SUCCESSFUL LEADERSHIP

Nothing is more important in your organization than the people you choose for its leadership.

He that walketh with wise men shall be wise: but a companion of fools shall be destroyed.

Proverbs 13:20 (KJV)

The above quotation is adapted from Rick Renner's book *If You Were God, Would You Choose You?*

But we have this treasure in earthen vessels, that the excellency of the power may be of God, and not of us.

2 Corinthians 4:7 (KJV)

We live in vessels that are far from perfect, so we should not be surprised when imperfect vessels occasionally behave imperfectly.

The above quotation is adapted from Rick Renner's book *The Point of No Return: Tackling Your Next New Assignment With Courage and Common Sense.*

SUCCESSFUL LEADERSHIP

W hen choosing a leader, never forget that there are other fish in the sea and that you are not locked into one person. If the person you're working with doesn't want to get with the program and cooperate with you, there are a lot of potential leaders out there, just waiting to be tapped into.

And they all with one consent began to make excuse... [The Lord said] ...None of those men which were bidden shall taste of my supper.

Luke 14:18,24 (KJV)

The above quotation is adapted from Rick Renner's book
If You Were God, Would You Choose You?

SUCCESSFUL LEADERSHIP

Desire is that insatiable urge, longing, appetite, craving, and yearning to stretch for something greater than you are right now.

The above quotation is adapted from Rick Renner's book *If You Were God, Would You Choose You?*

SUCCESSFUL LEADERSHIP

T hank God your promotion has not come quickly, for you would have not had the root, the depth, and the sure foundation to bear you up through the difficulties you will face when the mantle of leadership is passed on to you.

For it is God which worketh in you both to will and to do of his good pleasure.

Philippians 2:13 (KJV)

The above quotation is adapted from Rick Renner's book
The Point of No Return: Tackling Your Next New Assignment With Courage and Common Sense.

SUCCESSFUL LEADERSHIP

...Look not on his countenance, or on the height of his stature... for the Lord seeth not as man seeth; for man looketh on the outward appearance, but the Lord looketh on the heart.

1 Samuel 16:7 (KJV)

O ne of the greatest challenges for us in leadership is to not be led by what we see.

The above quotation is adapted from Rick Renner's book
If You Were God, Would You Choose You?

SUCCESSFUL LEADERSHIP

W hen a leader is guilty of chronic vacillation between projects, it should be no shock to him when his leadership team shuns the thought of another new idea. They don't believe that leader anymore! He's announced too many plans that he didn't fulfill.

A double minded man is unstable in all his ways.

James 1:8 (KJV)

The above quotation is adapted from Rick Renner's book *Who Is Ready for a Spiritual Promotion?*

SUCCESSFUL LEADERSHIP

Cast not away therefore your confidence, which hath great recompence of reward. For ye have need of patience, that after ye have done the will of God, ye might receive the promise.

Hebrews 10:35,36 (KJV)

If you don't allow anything to stop you — no matter what challenges the devil or life may try to throw at you — you will walk away with the respect and honor of others at the end of your battle. They'll see that yours wasn't a faith that tucked its tail and ran in rough times. They'll know that you stuck it out, and as a result, they will honor you for what you did!

The above quotation is adapted from Rick Renner's book *Who Is Ready for a Spiritual Promotion?*

SUCCESSFUL LEADERSHIP

U se this time in your life to prepare, change, and grow right now, so that when you are finally promoted and your dream becomes a reality, you'll have what you need internally to *keep* you in that place.

...See that you go on growing in the Lord, and become strong and vigorous in the truth you were taught.

Colossians 2:7 (TLB)

The above quotation is adapted from Rick Renner's book *The Point of No Return: Tackling Your Next New Assignment With Courage and Common Sense.*

Give not that which is holy unto the dogs, neither cast your pearls before swine....

Matthew 7:6 (KJV)

S top behaving like a beggar. You shouldn't have to beg anyone to follow you! You need to think more highly of yourself — and those who follow you need to think more highly of you as well.

The above quotation is adapted from Rick Renner's book
If You Were God, Would You Choose You?

SUCCESSFUL LEADERSHIP

If potential leaders are satisfied to live like pigs at home, that is probably the standard they will impart to their ministry or department.

For if a man know not how to rule his own house, how shall he take care of the church of God?

1 Timothy 3:5 (KJV)

The above quotation is adapted from Rick Renner's book *Who Is Ready for a Spiritual Promotion?*

I am pressing on to lay hold of that for which Christ Jesus has laid hold of me... forgetting what is in my past, I am pressing onward to take hold of the prize that is still before me....

Philippians 3:12,13 (REV)

To fulfill what God has planned for your life will require a fierce determination to keep moving ahead. Jogging along at a comfortable pace will never get you where you need to go. Achieving this goal will demand your utmost concentration, your undivided attention, and the empowerment of the Spirit of God.

The above quotation is adapted from Rick Renner's book *Sparkling Gems From the Greek.*

SUCCESSFUL LEADERSHIP

If your brain is so busy that you cannot hear what is being communicated, you will miss important details. Your inability to listen will cause you to make mistakes in your assignment. If you want to please your superior, it is essential to understand exactly what he wants.

Having eyes, do you not see [with them], and having ears, do you not hear and perceive and understand the sense of what is said? And do you not remember?

Mark 8:18 (AMP)

The above quotation is adapted from Rick Renner's book
Who Is Ready for a Spiritual Promotion?

SUCCESSFUL LEADERSHIP

Every man's work shall be made manifest: for the day will declare it, because it shall be revealed by fire; and the fire shall try every man's work of what sort it is.

1 Corinthians 3:13 (KJV)

If we build fast and cheaply when choosing our leadership, then that is what we're going to get — a fast, cheap work for God's Kingdom that fails when it encounters obstacles or opposition.

The above quotation is adapted from Rick Renner's book *If You Were God, Would You Choose You?*

I f we build slower but stronger, and if we build on the principles from God's Word, we will build a work that will survive all the storms of life that eventually come to test it.

He is like a man which built an house, and digged deep, and laid the foundation on a rock: and when the flood arose, the stream beat vehemently upon that house, and could not shake it: for it was founded upon a rock.

Luke 6:48 (KJV)

The above quotation is adapted from Rick Renner's book
If You Were God, Would You Choose You?

*...No man,
having put
his hand to the
plough, and
looking back,
is fit for the
kingdom of God.*

*Luke 9:62
(KJV)*

If you're so emotionally caught up in "the way it used to be" that you can't see how God wants it to be *now,* He may have to pass the baton from you to someone else. He is looking for someone who is willing to get up, get moving, and do what He wants done.

The above quotation is adapted from Rick Renner's book
Who Is Ready for a Spiritual Promotion?

SUCCESSFUL LEADERSHIP

Those who cultivate and develop the skill of listening make good team players because they're better able to understand other people's opinions and positions.

A wise man will hear, and will increase learning; and a man of understanding shall attain unto wise counsels.

Proverbs 1:5 (KJV)

The above quotation is adapted from Rick Renner's book
Who Is Ready for a Spiritual Promotion?

SUCCESSFUL LEADERSHIP

It is your job to pass this vital information to those under your authority. If you must, remind them about it again and again until you are sure they really heard the message you are trying to communicate to them.

1 Timothy 4:11 (REV)

To be a good communicator, you must make all the details of your plan clear so that people can easily follow you. *Followers need as much information as you can give them*. You'll need to tell them again and again and again. Spell it out and make it as plain as it can be. If you want people to follow your instructions, make those instructions so clear that they *cannot* be misinterpreted.

The above quotation is adapted from Rick Renner's book
Who Is Ready for a Spiritual Promotion?

SUCCESSFUL LEADERSHIP

There are very few quick successes in life. However, the ones who do achieve success instantly usually don't last very long because they haven't developed the maturity to *maintain* it.

...And because they had no root, they withered away.

Matthew 13:6 (KJV)

The above quotation is adapted from Rick Renner's book *The Point of No Return: Tackling Your Next New Assignment With Courage and Common Sense.*

SUCCESSFUL LEADERSHIP

[An overseer] must be one who manages his own household well....

1 Timothy 3:4 (NAS)

If a potential leader doesn't provide proper leadership at home, you have no reason to assume he can provide proper leadership to an entire department of the church, business, or organization.

The above quotation is adapted from Rick Renner's book
Who Is Ready for a Spiritual Promotion?

SUCCESSFUL LEADERSHIP

I f you choose leaders who share your heart and are submitted to your vision, they will be a blessing. But if you choose people who are not in agreement with what God has put in your heart, you will have invited a spiritual hurricane into your midst that has the power to destroy everything you have built. *So take the time to make sure you're making the right decision!*

Can two walk together, except they be agreed?

Amos 3:3 (KJV)

The above quotation is adapted from Rick Renner's book
If You Were God, Would You Choose You?

Instead, have a modest opinion of yourself, and learn to recognize the outstanding contributions that others have to impart.

Philippians 2:3 (REV)

R ather than incessantly talk and "hog" every conversation, we who are leaders must learn to make room for the gifts that lay resident in other people. Their talents and gifts are just as vital and important as ours.

The above quotation is adapted from Rick Renner's book *Sparkling Gems From the Greek.*

SUCCESSFUL LEADERSHIP

W hen hard times come, that isn't the time for you to surrender to your circumstances — it's time for you to put up a fight! That's when you need to "put up your dukes," heave backward with all your spiritual might, and throw a knockout punch at the face of the devil. Do something bold that will break that stranglehold the devil is trying to put on you!

Don't let bad circumstances wear you down and wear you out....

Galatians 6:9 (REV)

The above quotation is adapted from Rick Renner's book *Sparkling Gems From the Greek.*

SUCCESSFUL LEADERSHIP

And the Lord said, Who then is that faithful and wise steward, whom his lord shall make ruler over his household, to give them their portion of meat in due season?

Luke 12:42 (KJV)

If a potential leader can't take care of his own domain, why would you want to put him in charge of *your* domain? If his personal affairs are a mess, why do you think he would do better with *your* affairs?

The above quotation is adapted from Rick Renner's book *Who Is Ready for a Spiritual Promotion?*

SUCCESSFUL LEADERSHIP

A day of reckoning is coming in all of our futures when the books in Heaven will be opened. On that day, the Lord Jesus will look over the "profit-and-loss statement" for our lives, comparing what we did to what we were actually supposed to do.

After a long time the lord of those servants cometh, and reckoneth with them.

Matthew 25:19 (KJV)

The above quotation is adapted from Rick Renner's book *Sparkling Gems From the Greek*.

SUCCESSFUL LEADERSHIP

Let us hold fast to our confession — tightly wrapping our arms around it and embracing it with all our might — rejecting all attempts of anyone who tries to steal it away from us....

Hebrews 10:23 (REV)

When you finally discover God's will for your life — when His plan finally begins to awaken in your heart and you know exactly what you are to do — *hold fast* to that dream. Tightly embrace what God has shown you. Seize it — wrap your arms of faith around it. *Hold it down, and hold it tight!*

The above quotation is adapted from Rick Renner's book *Sparkling Gems From the Greek.*

SUCCESSFUL LEADERSHIP

H ow we build and the methods we use determine how long our work remains.

Every man's work shall be made manifest: for the day shall declare it, because it shall be revealed by fire; and the fire shall try every man's work of what sort it is.

1 Corinthians 3:13 (KJV)

SUCCESSFUL LEADERSHIP

Any enterprise is built by wise planning, becomes strong through common sense, and profits wonderfully by keeping abreast of the facts.

Proverbs 24:3,4 (TLB)

When you keep abreast of the facts, you know exactly where you are in terms of growth and progress. Staying ignorant of the facts is the fastest way to lose significant territory and to let another take your place of leadership.

The above quotation is adapted from Rick Renner's book *Who Is Ready for a Spiritual Promotion?*

H ow many lazy people do you know who are also successful?

...If anyone doesn't have enough gumption to get up, get a job, and go to work, then he shouldn't eat....

2 Thessalonians 3:10 (REV)

The above quotation is adapted from Rick Renner's book *The Point of No Return: Tackling Your Next New Assignment With Courage and Common Sense.*

For the time being no discipline brings joy, but seems grievous and painful; but afterwards it yields a peaceable fruit of righteousness to those who have been trained by it....

Hebrews 12:11 (AMP)

Nothing is more thrilling than to see progress in your own life. The path of growth often feels long and laborious, but afterward, when you can *see* and *appreciate* the results, you'll thank God that you didn't bail out!

The above quotation is adapted from Rick Renner's book *If You Were God, Would You Choose You?*

SUCCESSFUL LEADERSHIP

K nowing your limitations is just as important as knowing your potential.

But I say, through the grace given unto me, to every man that is among you, not to think of himself more highly than he ought to think; but to think soberly....

Romans 12:3 (KJV)

The above quotation is adapted from Rick Renner's book
The Point of No Return: Tackling Your Next New Assignment With Courage and Common Sense.

SUCCESSFUL LEADERSHIP

Where no counsel is, the people fall: but in the multitude of counsellors there is safety.

Proverbs 11:14 (KJV)

W hen leaders are afraid to let others in their organization take a leading role, they limit themselves and hinder the growth of their organization. Their control is *too strict* to allow for growth.

The above quotation is adapted from Rick Renner's book
Who Is Ready for a Spiritual Promotion?

SUCCESSFUL LEADERSHIP

W hen your inner belief system — *your sense of principle* — is so strong that you faithfully stand by it no matter what, you will occasionally find yourself on a collision course with the world and even with other believers who are less inclined to stand true to their convictions.

The integrity of the upright shall guide them....

Proverbs 11:3 (KJV)

The above quotation is adapted from Rick Renner's book *If You Were God, Would You Choose You?*

*Know ye not
that they which
run in a race run
all, but one
receiveth the prize?
So run, that ye
may obtain.*

1 Corinthians 9:24
(KJV)

The need for additional finances is so big and scary to some leaders that they often rationalize their own inaction, saying that the benefits of growth are too risky. Rather than press forward to achieve more, they retreat into a mode of self-preservation. For them, *maintaining* is more important than *gaining*.

The above quotation is adapted from Rick Renner's book
Who Is Ready for a Spiritual Promotion?

I t is easy to say you would give Jesus everything when He has never asked you for anything.

Now when Jesus heard these things, he said unto him, Yet lackest thou one thing: sell all that thou hast, and distribute unto the poor, and thou shalt have treasure in heaven: and come, follow me.

Luke 18:22 (KJV)

The above quotation is adapted from Rick Renner's book *The Point of No Return: Tackling Your Next New Assignment With Courage and Common Sense.*

I beseech you therefore, brethren, by the mercies of God, that ye present your bodies a living sacrifice, holy, acceptable unto God, which is your reasonable service.

Romans 12:1 (KJV)

Train yourself to begin each day with a prayer of consecration in which you solemnly and reverently present yourself and all you are to God. Don't assume that because you did it yesterday, you don't need to do it today. Each new day beckons you to take a step closer to the Lord and to make a commitment more serious than the one you made before.

The above quotation is adapted from Rick Renner's book *Sparkling Gems From the Greek.*

SUCCESSFUL LEADERSHIP

There have been many moments when my flesh screamed in disgust at the idea of discipline and commitment, but I knew I'd risk losing everything if I avoided the level of commitment God was asking of me.

No discipline seems pleasant at the time, but painful. Later on, however, it produces a harvest of righteousness and peace for those who have been trained by it.

Hebrews 12:11 (NIV)

The above quotation is adapted from Rick Renner's book
If You Were God, Would You Choose You?

So being affectionately desirous of you, we were willing to have imparted unto you, not the gospel of God only, but also our own souls, because ye were dear to us.

1 Thessalonians 2:8 (KJV)

People need leaders who are out in front leading the way, showing them step-by-step how to live successfully during both the challenging and prosperous times of life.

The above quotation is adapted from Rick Renner's book
Who Is Ready for a Spiritual Promotion?

SUCCESSFUL LEADERSHIP

T here is a concrete reason why some people succeed and others fail. A lack of preparation makes many people ill-equipped for the obstacles they will inevitably face along the way.

Study to shew thyself approved unto God, a workman that needeth not to be ashamed....

2 Timothy 2:15 (KJV)

The above quotation is adapted from Rick Renner's book *Who Is Ready for a Spiritual Promotion?*

*As vinegar to
the teeth and as
smoke to the eyes,
so is the sluggard
to those who
employ and
send him.*

*Proverbs 10:26
(AMP)*

D on't give someone a high-priority place of leadership on your team who stubbornly drags his feet and always resists change. This type of leader would only pull you down and keep your ministry or organization from making significant advances.

The above quotation is adapted from Rick Renner's book
Who Is Ready for a Spiritual Promotion?

SUCCESSFUL LEADERSHIP

W hen leaders get discouraged, that is often when they are tempted to walk away from it all. Unfortunately, many have walked away from their God-called position because of fleeting emotions in a moment of weakness. *Don't let that be you!*

Don't discard, dispel, dismiss, dump, or cast off your bold declaration of faith, because it has great recompense of reward.

Hebrews 10:35 (REV)

The above quotation is adapted from Rick Renner's book *Sparkling Gems From the Greek.*

SUCCESSFUL LEADERSHIP

For the eyes of the Lord run to and fro throughout the whole earth, to shew himself strong in the behalf of them whose heart is perfect toward him....

2 Chronicles 16:9 (KJV)

The Bible says that God's eyes are roaming, searching, running to and fro in the earth, seeking someone whose heart is right toward Him. The fact that God searches so *intensely* must mean that this kind of candidate is *not* found on every street!

SUCCESSFUL LEADERSHIP

How a person handles money is very revealing. It tells a lot about his personal integrity, his character, and how he respects the rights of others.

The just man walketh in his integrity: his children are blessed after him.

Proverbs 20:7 (KJV)

The above quotation is adapted from Rick Renner's book
Who Is Ready for a Spiritual Promotion?

For many are called, but few are chosen.

Matthew 22:14 (KJV)

God is not obliged to use everyone who prays, *"God, please use me!"* Neither are *you* obligated to use everyone who shows up and says he or she feels called to be a part of your team.

The above quotation is adapted from Rick Renner's book
If You Were God, Would You Choose You?

SUCCESSFUL LEADERSHIP

If you struggle with disorder, chaos, turmoil, confusion, upheaval, and anarchy in your private life, it will obviously affect your ability to carry on publicly as a leader.

To him who orders his way aright I shall show the salvation of God.

Psalm 50:23 (NAS)

The above quotation is adapted from Rick Renner's book *Who Is Ready for a Spiritual Promotion?*

SUCCESSFUL LEADERSHIP

And the Lord answered me, and said, Write the vision, and make it plain upon tables, that he may run that readeth it.

Habakkuk 2:2 (KJV)

Information is vital to any organization. It clears up misunderstandings. It gives a solid footing to move into the future. By giving his followers knowledge and understanding, a leader makes it easier for them to follow him. Most people will follow if they can see the goal, why they are going there, what the purpose is, and how much cost is involved. *A good leader must communicate all those facts.*

The above quotation is adapted from Rick Renner's book *Who Is Ready for a Spiritual Promotion?*

SUCCESSFUL LEADERSHIP

When circumstances try to knock you out of your assignment, you must have a fierce, unwavering commitment that you are not going to leave where God has called you.

But without faith it is impossible to please him: for he that cometh to God must believe that he is, and that he is a rewarder of them that diligently seek him.

Hebrews 11:6 (KJV)

The above quotation is adapted from Rick Renner's book *Sparkling Gems From the Greek*.

Depart from evil, and do good; seek peace, and pursue it.

Psalm 34:14 (KJV)

D o what is right. Let this be your guiding principle when selecting leadership.

The above quotation is adapted from Rick Renner's book *If You Were God, Would You Choose You?*

SUCCESSFUL LEADERSHIP

I f you are mightily anointed by God, it is simply a fact that your schedule will get busier, your demands will increase, and your challenges will grow. But as long as you allow God to develop your character along the way, you will find that you're able to successfully manage anything He puts on your plate!

For unto every one that hath shall be given, and he shall have abundance....

Matthew 25:29 (KJV)

The above quotation is adapted from Rick Renner's book
Sparkling Gems From the Greek.

SUCCESSFUL LEADERSHIP

And the Lord said unto Samuel, How long wilt thou mourn for Saul, seeing I have rejected him.... fill thine horn with oil, and go, I will send thee to Jesse the Bethlehemite, for I have provided me a king among his sons.

1 Samuel 16:1 (KJV)

Quit acting like the world rises and falls on whether or not one person gets with the program. If that person is not willing to fulfill his responsibility, then it's time to move on to someone who will contribute to your vision instead of being a *taker* and a *consumer* of your time and energy.

The above quotation is adapted from Rick Renner's book
If You Were God, Would You Choose You?

SUCCESSFUL LEADERSHIP

A s a leader, you must accept the fact that bringing correction to people under your sphere of authority is part of your God-given responsibility. As you seek the mind of the Lord, the Holy Spirit will show you how to speak to people in this situation and how to help them see what they need to change in their lives and attitudes so they can move up higher in God.

Be shepherds of God's flock that is under your care, serving as overseers...not lording it over those entrusted to you, but being examples to the flock.

1 Peter 5:2,3 (NIV)

The above quotation is adapted from Rick Renner's book *Sparkling Gems From the Greek.*

SUCCESSFUL LEADERSHIP

...He that hearkeneth unto counsel is wise.

Proverbs 12:15 (KJV)

L istening to your team members' opinions not only helps you, but it lets them know that their input is important and pulls them into the decision-making process. And because they have helped you make the decision, they share with you a sense of responsibility about that decision.

The above quotation is adapted from Rick Renner's book *Who Is Ready for a Spiritual Promotion?*

SUCCESSFUL LEADERSHIP

W hen the harvest is ready to be reaped, don't be threatened by people who come later to join you in the reaping process. The fact is that it requires many more hands to reap than it does to sow.

The above quotation is adapted from Rick Renner's book *Sparkling Gems From the Greek.*

SUCCESSFUL LEADERSHIP

One thing is for sure: People are not chosen by accident. Names were not scribbled on paper, thrown into a big brown bag, shaken up, and pulled out of the pile. If God chooses us, He does so because He sees something inside us that qualifies us to be a part of His team.

The above quotation is adapted from Rick Renner's book
If You Were God, Would You Choose You?

D isrespectful children are usually an indicator of a serious problem in the home. At church, everyone may dress beautifully and smile just right, but if there is disrespect between parents and their children, it's usually (though not always) a warning signal that the home is out of order.

[A leader] must rule his own household well, keeping his children under control, with true dignity, commanding their respect in every way and keeping them respectful.

1 Timothy 3:4 (AMP)

The above quotation is adapted from Rick Renner's book
Who Is Ready for a Spiritual Promotion?

Ye have compassed this mountain long enough....

Deuteronomy 2:3 (KJV)

A major tool the devil uses to keep people from achieving the big victories is to get them stuck on small victories. They are so proud of what they've done that they camp out at a low-level victory. They stop at the foothills when the highest mountain peaks are still before them.

The above quotation is adapted from Rick Renner's book
If You Were God, Would You Choose You?

If you really want to know where a person's heart is, follow his money and you'll find out. *Money tells the truth!*

For where your treasure is, there your heart will be also.

Matthew 6:21 (NIV)

The above quotation is adapted from Rick Renner's book *Who Is Ready for a Spiritual Promotion?*

...But be thou an example of the believers, in word, in conversation, in charity, in spirit, in faith, in purity.

1 Timothy 4:12 (KJV)

Knowing how to treat people is part of a responsible leader's job. Those who possess this quality are well-esteemed among their followers. On the other hand, those who show no courtesy for others are usually not well thought of.

The above quotation is adapted from Rick Renner's book *Who Is Ready for a Spiritual Promotion?*

SUCCESSFUL LEADERSHIP

Accomplishing tasks in a manner that is right, even if it is slower, never hurts your church or organization. By taking this approach, you may not gain ground as quickly as you wished; but when you finally gain that ground, it will *really* be yours.

Whatever may be your task, work at it heartily (from the soul), as [something done] for the Lord and not for men.

Colossians 3:23 (AMP)

The above quotation is adapted from Rick Renner's book *If You Were God, Would You Choose You?*

But let patience have her perfect work. I'm talking about the kind of attitude that hangs in there, never giving up, refusing to surrender to obstacles and turning down every opportunity to quit....

James 1:4 (REV)

Patience is needed for you to outlast any difficulty, time of stress, or pressure that comes your way. Make up your mind that you're going to stand your ground and hang in there. It won't be long until the problems flee — and when they do, you'll be so glad you didn't give up.

The above quotation is adapted from Rick Renner's book *Sparkling Gems From the Greek.*

SUCCESSFUL LEADERSHIP

R ather than trying to figure out everything by yourself, why don't you let
the people around you contribute their
thoughts, views, and insights? You'll discover
that you can accomplish a whole lot more as
a team than you can do by yourself.

For I say,
through the grace
given unto me,
to every man that
is among you, not
to think of himself
more highly
than he ought
to think....

Romans 12:3
(KJV)

The above quotation is adapted from Rick Renner's book
Sparkling Gems From the Greek.

SUCCESSFUL LEADERSHIP

*Seeing then that
we have such
hope, we use
great plainness
of speech.*

2 Corinthians 3:12
(KJV)

When staff members misunderstand their leader's instructions 99% of the time, something is wrong with the way that leader is communicating with those under his authority. His followers *cannot* be wrong all the time.

The above quotation is adapted from Rick Renner's book
Who Is Ready for a Spiritual Promotion?

SUCCESSFUL LEADERSHIP

Y ou can be sure that plenty of adverse circumstances will arise to tempt you to compromise what you believe and what you are doing.

The light shines in darkness, but the darkness did not have the ability to suppress or hold the light under its domain.

John 1:5 (REV)

The above quotation is adapted from Rick Renner's book *If You Were God, Would You Choose You?*

Whatever you do, work at it with all your heart, as working for the Lord, not for men.

Colossians 3:23 (NIV)

Rather than contesting your present assignment and complaining about it all the time, jump in with both feet! Give it everything you've got! *Do the best you can!*

The above quotation is adapted from Rick Renner's book
If You Were God, Would You Choose You?

SUCCESSFUL LEADERSHIP

I f you can't repeat your superior's instructions back to him, you probably didn't understand them in the first place. So if there is something you don't understand, take the time to ask for clarification. Your superior will appreciate it, and it will save loads of time and mistakes later on down the road.

A wise man will hear, and will increase learning....

Proverbs 1:5 (KJV)

The above quotation is adapted from Rick Renner's book *Who Is Ready for a Spiritual Promotion?*

*But God
hath chosen the
foolish things
of the world to
confound the wise;
and God hath
chosen the weak
things of the
world to confound
the things which
are mighty.*

*1 Corinthians 1:27
(KJV)*

The very thing that you think should disqualify you may actually be what makes you a *first pick* in God's mind.

The above quotation is adapted from Rick Renner's book
If You Were God, Would You Choose You?

SUCCESSFUL LEADERSHIP

T ake notice when you find people who demonstrate loyalty and a fierce determination to be used in your ministry; who refuse to be easily moved; and who will *not* give up. This may be an indicator that they possess the kind of desire you want in your leaders.

But you know that Timothy has proven himself, because as a son with his father he has served with me in the work of the gospel.

Philippians 2:22 (NIV)

The above quotation is adapted from Rick Renner's book *Who Is Ready for a Spiritual Promotion?*

SUCCESSFUL LEADERSHIP

...Well done, thou good and faithful servant; thou hast been faithful over a few things, I will make thee ruler over many things....

Matthew 25:21 (KJV)

G od entrusts great power only to those who have proven themselves faithful.

The above quotation is adapted from Rick Renner's book *Who Is Ready for a Spiritual Promotion?*

SUCCESSFUL LEADERSHIP

Y ou need to know for yourself that you are mature enough to move on to the next level. If the next job assignment is too big and comes too quickly, you won't have peace as you enter into it.

But don't begin until you count the cost....

Luke 14:28 (TLB)

The above quotation is adapted from Rick Renner's book
If You Were God, Would You Choose You?

Iron sharpeneth iron; so a man sharpeneth the countenance of his friend.

Proverbs 27:17 (KJV)

When people begin working together in a close environment, sparks of strife sometimes ignite when wills or personalities collide or when people hold different opinions about a particular subject or direction to be taken. These collision points help to reveal whether or not people possess the compatibility to work together on one team.

The above quotation is adapted from Rick Renner's book *Who Is Ready for a Spiritual Promotion?*

SUCCESSFUL LEADERSHIP

D ealing with the flesh is like chastening a child. The flesh must be controlled, corrected, and made to obey, even if it wants to do otherwise. It must be told what to do and made to obey. The process is painful, but the rewards are eternal.

Let not sin therefore reign in your mortal body, that ye should obey it in the lusts thereof.

Romans 6:12 (KJV)

The above quotation is adapted from Rick Renner's book
If You Were God, Would You Choose You?

SUCCESSFUL LEADERSHIP

Wherefore by their fruits ye shall know them.

Matthew 7:20 (KJV)

T alents and gifts are important, but they do not supercede the importance of a person's character!

The above quotation is adapted from Rick Renner's book
Sparkling Gems From the Greek.

D on't feel let down or discouraged when you discover weaknesses in your fellow team members' personalities. Remember that they have probably encountered a few surprises in your personality too!

Judge not,
that ye be
not judged.

Matthew 7:1
(KJV)

The above quotation is adapted from Rick Renner's book
Who Is Ready for a Spiritual Promotion?

For God so loved the world, that he gave his only begotten Son, that whosoever believeth in him should not perish, but have ever-lasting life.

John 3:16 (KJV)

Nothing in the world is more valuable or precious than the people of God.

The above quotation is adapted from Rick Renner's book
If You Were God, Would You Choose You?

SUCCESSFUL LEADERSHIP

M any leaders are afraid to obey what the Holy Spirit puts in their hearts to do. Fearful that they will be led astray or that they will make a mistake, they sit on the sidelines and watch other people achieve success, while they remain right where they've always been.

Howbeit when he, the Spirit of truth, is come, he will guide you into all truth....

John 16:13 (KJV)

The above quotation is adapted from Rick Renner's book *Sparkling Gems From the Greek*.

So then because thou art lukewarm, and neither cold nor hot, I will spue thee out of my mouth.

Revelation 3:16 (KJV)

M ediocre standards are *not* normal.

The above quotation is adapted from Rick Renner's book
Who Is Ready for a Spiritual Promotion?

SUCCESSFUL LEADERSHIP

We live in a world that has thrown principle to the wind. More often than not, a wimpish world chooses not to stick to what is right. Regretfully, even believers and spiritual leaders are often wimpish, quickly succumbing to other people's opinions and other sources of outside pressures.

Only be thou strong and very courageous, that thou mayest observe to do according to all the law...turn not from it to the right hand or to the left, that thou mayest prosper whithersoever thou goest.

Joshua 1:7 (KJV)

The above quotation is adapted from Rick Renner's book
If You Were God, Would You Choose You?

The integrity of the upright shall guide them....

Proverbs 11:3 (KJV)

P rinciple is a person's inward rule. It is a conviction of what is right and wrong; a moral foundation that determines how one sees and responds to life; a rock-solid belief system so ingrained into one's disposition that he cannot ignore or deviate from it.

The above quotation is adapted from Rick Renner's book *If You Were God, Would You Choose You?*

SUCCESSFUL LEADERSHIP

R efusing to budge, unwilling to give an inch, a belligerent person can put an entire group and project "on hold" because of a stubborn, quarrelsome attitude. When everyone else is in agreement about a project and ready to get moving, this kind of negative attitude is a terrific irritant.

Some among you have become like a bone out of joint — a source of real pain and irritation to the whole body.

1 Timothy 1:6 (REV)

The above quotation is adapted from Rick Renner's book *Sparkling Gems From the Greek*.

SUCCESSFUL LEADERSHIP

*Where there
is no vision,
the people are
unrestrained....*

*Proverbs 29:18
(NAS)*

W here there is a vacuum of leadership, instability is the result.

The above quotation is adapted from Rick Renner's book
*The Point of No Return: Tackling Your Next New Assignment
With Courage and Common Sense.*

SUCCESSFUL LEADERSHIP

I f you want to be great or to do great things, you must learn to be *constant, stable, dependable, inflexible, unbending,* and *unyielding* in the face of challenges. This is a common characteristic shared by all great achievers. You see, there will be many attacks that will try to pull you off course, so your commitment to stay on track is absolutely essential.

...Be constant, stable, enduring, and dependable....

1 Corinthians 15:58 (REV)

The above quotation is adapted from Rick Renner's book *The Point of No Return: Tackling Your Next New Assignment With Courage and Common Sense.*

*Kings take
pleasure in
honest lips;
they value a man
who speaks
the truth.*

*Proverbs 16:13
(NIV)*

Most people hate to fill out forms and give reports. But a person's ability, or lack thereof, to keep you regularly and faithfully informed is a key factor in determining whether or not he or she is fit for leadership.

The above quotation is adapted from Rick Renner's book
Who Is Ready for a Spiritual Promotion?

SUCCESSFUL LEADERSHIP

B efore we open our hearts and begin to share our deepest experiences and most precious inner treasures, we need to be certain that we are talking to people who are serious about their walk with God. Our time and treasures are too precious to throw at the feet of people who don't care and who won't apply what we are trying to tell them.

Never invest too much time, energy, or money into people who don't even care about what you are doing for them!

Matthew 7:6 (REV)

The above quotation is adapted from Rick Renner's book *Sparkling Gems From the Greek*.

SUCCESSFUL LEADERSHIP

S elf-deception is very costly. Telling yourself everything is all right when it isn't may temporarily relieve you from the pain of having to look at the facts head-on. But in the end, ignoring the facts will cost you so much more in terms of time, heartbreak, and defeat.

The above quotation is adapted from Rick Renner's book *Sparkling Gems From the Greek*.

W ake up! Sitting around and hoping for something to happen isn't going to produce anything! You have to jump in the race, fix your eyes on the goal, and run with all your might to the finish line so you can take the prize!

Know ye not that they which run in a race run all, but one receiveth the prize? So run, that ye may obtain.

1 Corinthians 9:24 (KJV)

The above quotation is adapted from Rick Renner's book *Sparkling Gems From the Greek*.

Have I not commanded thee? Be strong and of a good courage....

Joshua 1:9 (KJV)

Y ou are a leader! You don't have the privilege of showing the same kind of weakness that other people show.

The above quotation is adapted from Rick Renner's book
The Point of No Return: Tackling Your Next New Assignment With Courage and Common Sense.

SUCCESSFUL LEADERSHIP

I would rather work with a less talented person who has *desire* than with a talented person who has *no* desire. It's better to train a young man or woman who doesn't have a lot of experience and is less qualified than others, but who is willing to pay the price, put in the time and effort, and make personal sacrifices to become all that he or she can be.

...The precious possession of a man is diligence.

Proverbs 12:27 (NAS)

The above quotation is adapted from Rick Renner's book *Who Is Ready for a Spiritual Promotion?*

SUCCESSFUL LEADERSHIP

Be of good courage, and let us behave ourselves valiantly for our people, and for the cities of our God: and let the Lord do that which is good in his sight.

1 Chronicles 19:13
(KJV)

If anything is needed today, it is leaders who are willing to take a stand and who are willing to do what is right, regardless of whether or not it is politically correct. Leaders who are *strong* and *courageous* are very scarce, both in the world and in the Church.

The above quotation is adapted from Rick Renner's book
The Point of No Return: Tackling Your Next New Assignment With Courage and Common Sense.

W hat is on the *inside* of a person you are considering for promotion determines what you're really going to get!

Even so every good tree bringeth forth good fruit; but a corrupt tree bringeth forth evil fruit.

Matthew 7:17 (KJV)

The above quotation is adapted from Rick Renner's book
If You Were God, Would You Choose You?

Rather, let our lives lovingly express truth [in all things, speaking truly, dealing truly, living truly]....

Ephesians 4:15 (AMP)

How we view ourselves is often not how others view us. Getting a second opinion is sometimes useful (and sometimes painful) in helping us ascertain what we are really contributing to the team.

The above quotation is adapted from Rick Renner's book *Who Is Ready for a Spiritual Promotion?*

SUCCESSFUL LEADERSHIP

W hen you are a leader, there is a time for you to keep your mouth shut and to put on a happy face, even if you don't feel happy.

To everything there is a season, and a time to every purpose under the heaven... a time to weep, and a time to laugh; a time to mourn, and a time to dance.

Ecclesiastes 3:1,4 (KJV)

The above quotation is adapted from Rick Renner's book
*The Point of No Return: Tackling Your Next New Assignment
With Courage and Common Sense.*

SUCCESSFUL LEADERSHIP

A man's gift maketh room for him, and bringeth him before great men.

Proverbs 18:16 (KJV)

Don't get frustrated if you feel like your superiors are holding you back from the advancement you desire. It is wise for them to take the time to know you, to test you, and to make sure that you are the right candidate for the job.

The above quotation is adapted from Rick Renner's book *If You Were God, Would You Choose You?*

SUCCESSFUL LEADERSHIP

Unrealistic expectations — whether placed on leaders by followers, or on followers by leaders — always lead to disappointment. It's better to avoid disappointment by keeping a realistic view of people.

Therefore from now on we recognize no man according to the flesh....

2 Corinthians 5:16 (NAS)

The above quotation is adapted from Rick Renner's book *Who Is Ready for a Spiritual Promotion?*

God has picked out people whom the world thinks are laughable, and through them He is confounding those who think they are so high and mighty....

1 Corinthians 1:28 (REV)

Take a look at world history and you'll see that God *hasn't* primarily specialized in using kings, queens, royalty, politicians, scientists, philosophers, writers, movie stars, or celebrities to advance His Kingdom.

The above quotation is adapted from Rick Renner's book *If You Were God, Would You Choose You?*

SUCCESSFUL LEADERSHIP

Anytime something small becomes a *major issue,* you need to back up and reexamine what you are thinking and feeling. The devil may be trying to work in your mind and imagination to divide you from people you both love and need. *Do you want the devil to build a wall between you and the people in your life over something that won't even matter a year from now?*

Neither give place to the devil.

Ephesians 4:27 (KJV)

The above quotation is adapted from Rick Renner's book *Sparkling Gems From the Greek.*

...For He is like a refiner's fire, and like fullers' soap: and he shall sit as a refiner and purifier of silver....

Malachi 3:2,3 (KJV)

If God placed you in a powerful position without first removing the dross from your life, that defect would show up later and cripple your work or ministry. Therefore, thank God for the fiery experiences that cause you to see the character defects in your life so they can be dealt with and removed.

The above quotation is adapted from Rick Renner's book *If You Were God, Would You Choose You?*

SUCCESSFUL LEADERSHIP

I f you're going to fulfill the dream God has given you, you will have to learn how to cooperate with other key people — *your partners in life* — who can assist you in fulfilling that dream.

Two are better than one; because they have a good reward for their labour. For if they fall, the one will lift up his fellow: but woe to him that is alone when he falleth; for he hath not another to help him up.

Ecclesiastes 4:9,10 (KJV)

The above quotation is adapted from Rick Renner's book *Sparkling Gems From the Greek*.

SUCCESSFUL LEADERSHIP

And this shall be a sign unto you; Ye shall find the babe wrapped in swaddling clothes, lying in a manger.

Luke 2:12 (KJV)

G od has always shown up in places where He wasn't expected.

The above quotation is adapted from Rick Renner's book *If You Were God, Would You Choose You?*

SUCCESSFUL LEADERSHIP

There is no law of gravity powerful enough to permanently hold down a person's thoughts, feelings, and convictions. Even if that person tries to hide his real feelings and attitudes, sooner or later they will be revealed by his words and actions.

...Out of the abundance of the heart the mouth speaketh.

Matthew 12:34 (KJV)

The above quotation is adapted from Rick Renner's book *Who Is Ready for a Spiritual Promotion?*

The desire of the sluggard puts him to death, for his hands refuse to work.

Proverbs 21:25 (NAS)

Y ou can send people to school, educate them, and even pay for them to fly halfway around the world in order to learn new and better techniques. But if they don't possess the inner drive to become better and more professional, it doesn't matter how much time or money you throw at them. It's all a waste unless they have *desire*.

The above quotation is adapted from Rick Renner's book *Who Is Ready for a Spiritual Promotion?*

SUCCESSFUL LEADERSHIP

J ust because you have an empty
position doesn't mean you have to
immediately find someone to fill it.

...[Jesus] went out into a mountain to pray, and continued all night in prayer to God. And when it was day...he chose twelve, whom also he named apostles.

Luke 6:12,13 (KJV)

The above quotation is adapted from Rick Renner's book
If You Were God, Would You Choose You?

Know ye not that they which run in a race run all, but only one receiveth the prize? So run, that ye may obtain.

1 Corinthians 9:24 (KJV)

Y ou must have resolve, strength of will, determination, backbone, high morale, courage, dedication, persistence, tenacity, and an unrelenting mindset. You must put your foot down and take your stand as a no-nonsense kind of person who puts your *whole heart* into your calling!

The above quotation is adapted from Rick Renner's book *Sparkling Gems From the Greek*.

SUCCESSFUL LEADERSHIP

L et me look at a person's finances, and in just a matter of minutes I can tell you what the most important thing is in his life. The way he spends his money will tell the whole story of what he prizes, cherishes, loves, and adores.

For where your treasure is, there will your heart be also.

Matthew 6:21 (KJV)

The above quotation is adapted from Rick Renner's book
Who Is Ready for a Spiritual Promotion?

SUCCESSFUL LEADERSHIP

If ye be willing and obedient, ye shall eat the good of the land.

Isaiah 1:19 (KJV)

A willingness to learn — to try new things and develop new approaches to life — is a *requirement* for anyone who wants to succeed in life.

The above quotation is adapted from Rick Renner's book *If You Were God, Would You Choose You?*

I f you own a business, set goals for your staff and sales people. Don't expect them to be the visionaries of your company. You are their leader! They need your vision, your faith, and your ideas about the future. Help them see where your company is headed and what the dividends will be for those who are faithful.

Then the Lord answered me and said, "Record the vision and inscribe it on tablets, that the one who reads it may run."

Habakkuk 2:2 (NAS)

The above quotation is adapted from Rick Renner's book *The Point of No Return: Tackling Your Next New Assignment With Courage and Common Sense.*

Pray without ceasing.

1 Thessalonians 5:17 (NAS)

Prayer is essential to making your vision happen. Not only is it the only way you are going to know the specific boundaries and perimeters of your vision, but it is the only way you can find out how, when, where, and with whom you are to proceed.

The above quotation is adapted from Rick Renner's book *The Point of No Return: Tackling Your Next New Assignment With Courage and Common Sense.*

G od puts those whom He chooses through a process designed to remove any weaknesses that could later create defects in their ministries or life assignments.

It was a lengthy process and I went through a lot of refining fires to get to this place, but finally I passed the test and God saw that I was genuinely ready....

1 Thessalonians 2:4 (REV)

The above quotation is adapted from Rick Renner's book
If You Were God, Would You Choose You?

SUCCESSFUL LEADERSHIP

...For whatsoever a man soweth, that shall he also reap.

Galatians 6:7 (KJV)

Y ou'll never become someone great or achieve anything extraordinarily special by doing exactly what everyone else does. If you want to stand above the rest of the crowd, you'll have to do something that the rest of the crowd isn't doing!

The above quotation is adapted from Rick Renner's book *Sparkling Gems From the Greek*.

W hat you fear or respect will affect the decisions you make!

The fear of man bringeth a snare: but whoso putteth his trust in the Lord shall be safe.

Proverbs 25:25 (KJV)

The above quotation is adapted from Rick Renner's book *The Point of No Return: Tackling Your Next New Assignment With Courage and Common Sense.*

Work hard and cheerfully at all you do, just as though you were working for the Lord and not merely for your masters.

Colossians 3:23 (TLB)

A ny person who does just the required minimum should *never* be considered for a position of leadership.

The above quotation is adapted from Rick Renner's book
Who Is Ready for a Spiritual Promotion?

SUCCESSFUL LEADERSHIP

M any big churches, ministries, and corporations lost the cutting edge they once held because they spent most of their energy gloating about how big and good they were. While they were gloating about the past, another smaller church or organization with excited and dedicated people and a huge vision snuck up from behind and *surpassed* them!

Brethren, I count not myself to have apprehended: but this one thing I do, forgetting those things which are behind, and reaching forth unto those things which are before.

Philippians 3:13 (KJV)

The above quotation is adapted from Rick Renner's book *Sparkling Gems From the Greek.*

SUCCESSFUL LEADERSHIP

Thou wilt surely wear away, both thou, and this people that is with thee: for this thing is too heavy for thee; thou art not able to perform it thyself alone.

Exodus 18:18 (KJV)

A leader's arms can only reach so far. Therefore, if he doesn't have good helpers to stand at his side and assist him, he'll never be able to oversee an organization that grows beyond his reach.

The above quotation is adapted from Rick Renner's book *Sparkling Gems From the Greek.*

SUCCESSFUL LEADERSHIP

I have learned through the years that a person who is content to live an average, run-of-the-mill, non-productive life will never be mightily used by God.

Do you see a man skilled in his work? He will stand before kings; he will not stand before obscure men.

Proverbs 22:29 (NAS)

The above quotation is adapted from Rick Renner's book *If You Were God, Would You Choose You?*

SUCCESSFUL LEADERSHIP

...He who is hasty of spirit exposes and exalts his folly.

Proverbs 14:29 (AMP)

Whenever leaders act too hastily and make decisions under pressure, they often make decisions they later regret.

The above quotation is adapted from Rick Renner's book *If You Were God, Would You Choose You?*

SUCCESSFUL LEADERSHIP

L et's face it — it's extremely difficult to do everything simultaneously. You may be able to do it for a while. But in time, you'll start missing important details, forgetting what you said, missing appointments, messing up your finances, and even getting emotional over unemotional issues because you've pushed yourself beyond your limit. If this is you, *slow down* and set aside some time to be with the Lord.

Be still, and know that I am God....

Psalm 46:10 (KJV)

The above quotation is adapted from Rick Renner's book *Sparkling Gems From the Greek*.

SUCCESSFUL LEADERSHIP

Come unto me, all ye that labour and are heavy laden, and I will give you rest.

Matthew 11:28 (KJV)

It's better to wait and be temporarily inconvenienced than to hastily install a wrong person into a leadership position and then later have to figure out a way to remove him.

The above quotation is adapted from Rick Renner's book *Sparkling Gems From the Greek*.

SUCCESSFUL LEADERSHIP

I f you want to be used in a leadership capacity, do not despise where you are right now. What you are doing may seem small and insignificant, but the actions, attitudes, and faithfulness you demonstrate right now will become the foundation for your future usefulness to God and to your leaders.

The above quotation is adapted from Rick Renner's book
Who Is Ready for a Spiritual Promotion?

SUCCESSFUL LEADERSHIP

Take pains with these things; be absorbed in them, so that your progress may be evident to all.

1 Timothy 4:15 (NAS)

I f you're serious about being successful, then you'll have to give your full attention to whatever God has called you to do. Your task must have your full consideration, your undivided attention, and your mental and spiritual concentration. Distractions are *not* allowed.

The above quotation is adapted from Rick Renner's book *Sparkling Gems From the Greek*.

SUCCESSFUL LEADERSHIP

T he only way we can remain continually effective is by making sure we spend time with the Lord. To think that we are going to run into the Lord's Presence and get everything we need in the space of five minutes isn't realistic. *We must schedule time to be alone with God.*

But thou, when thou prayest, enter into thy closet, and when thou hast shut thy door, pray to thy Father which is in secret....

Matthew 6:6 (KJV)

The above quotation is adapted from Rick Renner's book *Sparkling Gems From the Greek*.

Enlarge the place of thy tent, and let them stretch forth the curtains of thy habitations; spare not, lengthen thy cords, and strengthen thy stakes.

Isaiah 54:2 (KJV)

If your church, ministry, or organization doesn't have to deal with the challenges of growth, it is a signal that something is obviously unhealthy in the organization.

The above quotation is adapted from Rick Renner's book
Who Is Ready for a Spiritual Promotion?

SUCCESSFUL LEADERSHIP

Search high and low for people who read books, listen to teaching tapes, and attend seminars to learn how to perform their responsibilities and improve their skills. Choose those who strive for excellence in the way they live, where they live, and how they dress.

Happy is the man that findeth wisdom, and the man that getteth understanding. For the merchandise of it is better than the merchandise of silver, and the gain thereof than fine gold.

Proverbs 3:13,14 (KJV)

The above quotation is adapted from Rick Renner's book *If You Were God, Would You Choose You?*

Rejoice with them that do rejoice, and weep with them that weep.

Romans 12:15 (KJV)

L earning to respond with appropriate emotions is very important. We need to be sensitive to the needs of those around us, allowing the Holy Spirit to show us how to respond to the emotional climate in which we find ourselves.

The above quotation is adapted from Rick Renner's book *Sparkling Gems From the Greek*.

SUCCESSFUL LEADERSHIP

G od wants to use everyone, but everyone will not be used.

For many are called, but few are chosen.

Matthew 22:14 (KJV)

The above quotation is adapted from Rick Renner's book
If You Were God, Would You Choose You?

*Thou therefore
endure hardness,
as a good soldier
of Jesus Christ.*

*2 Timothy 2:3
(KJV)*

T he difficulty of the task does not change the *necessity* of the task!

The above quotation is adapted from Rick Renner's book
Who Is Ready for a Spiritual Promotion?

SUCCESSFUL LEADERSHIP

I f you choose a passionless, desireless person to run a division of your church, ministry, business, or organization, it won't be long until that division of your ministry or business becomes *sluggish* and *non-performing*. Even worse than that, the person you placed in charge will be *content* with the results!

As the door turneth upon his hinges, so doth the slothful upon his bed.

Proverbs 26:14 (KJV)

The above quotation is adapted from Rick Renner's book
If You Were God, Would You Choose You?

*Bless them
which persecute
you: bless, and
curse not.*

*Romans 12:14
(KJV)*

Never underestimate the importance of how you react to those who wrong you. Your words of blessing and forgiveness can put to bed forever all the past wrongs ever committed against you. On the other hand, your words of retaliation can reignite the fire of opposition so that the same kind of attack keeps reoccurring again and again.

The above quotation is adapted from Rick Renner's book *Sparkling Gems From the Greek.*

SUCCESSFUL LEADERSHIP

Your calling and convictions will put you at odds with others from time to time. Therefore, if you aren't guided by an *inward conviction* to stand by *your principles,* the devil will use others to sway you from what you know to be true and right.

Therefore, my beloved brethren, be steadfast, immovable, always abounding in the work of the Lord....

1 Corinthians 15:58 (NAS)

The above quotation is adapted from Rick Renner's book
If You Were God, Would You Choose You?

SUCCESSFUL LEADERSHIP

In this case, moreover, it is required of stewards that one be found trustworthy.

1 Corinthians 4:2 (NAS)

Trust is the key for the expansion of any organization.

The above quotation is adapted from Rick Renner's book *If You Were God, Would You Choose You?*

About Rick Renner

Rick Renner is a highly respected leader and teacher within the global Christian community. He ministered widely throughout the United States for many years before answering God's call in 1991 to move his family to the former Soviet Union and plunge into the heart of its newly emerging Church.

Following an apostolic call on his life, Rick works alongside his wife Denise to see the Gospel preached, leadership trained, and the Church established throughout the world. Today Rick's broadcast "Good News With Rick Renner" reaches a potential audience of more than 100 million viewers who reside in the former Soviet Union. He has distributed hundreds of thousands of teaching audio and videotapes, and his best-selling books have been translated into five major languages — Spanish, Portuguese, French, Russian, and German — as well as multiple other languages that are spoken in the former USSR.

Rick is founder of the *Good News Association of Churches and Ministries,* through which he assists and strengthens almost 700 churches in the territory of the former Soviet Union. He also pastors the fast-growing *Moscow Good News Church,* located in the very heart of Moscow, Russia.

Books by Rick Renner

Books in English

Seducing Spirits and Doctrines of Demons

Living in the Combat Zone

Merchandising the Anointing

Dressed To Kill

Spiritual Weapons To Defeat the Enemy

Dream Thieves

The Point of No Return

The Dynamic Duo

If You Were God, Would You Choose You?

Who Is Ready for a Spiritual Promotion?

It's Time for You To Fulfill Your Secret Dreams

Isn't It Time for You To Get Over It?

Sparkling Gems From the Greek Daily Devotional

Insights on Successful Leadership

Insights on Spiritual Warfare

Books in Russian

How To Test Spiritual Manifestations

Living in the Combat Zone

Merchandising the Anointing

Dressed To Kill

Spiritual Weapons To Defeat the Enemy

Dream Thieves

The Point of No Return

The Dynamic Duo

Hell Is a Real Place

What the Bible Says About Water Baptism

What the Bible Says About Tithes and Offerings

What the Bible Says About the Devil

Signs of the Second Coming of Jesus Christ

It's Time for You To Fulfill Your Secret Dreams

Isn't It Time for You To Get Over It?

Who Is Ready for a Spiritual Promotion?

The Death, Burial, and Resurrection of Jesus Christ

Insights on Successful Leadership

Insights on Spiritual Warfare

For Further Information

For all book orders, please contact:

Teach All Nations
*A book company anointed to take God's Word
to you and to the nations of the world.*

A Division of
Rick Renner Ministries
P. O. Box 702040
Tulsa, OK 74170-2040
Phone: 877-281-8644
Fax: 918-496-3278
Email: renner@renner.org

*To order a complete audio, video, and book catalog,
please contact our offices in Tulsa, Oklahoma.*